MODERN TOSS BOOK

*from *hitflap*

by Jon Link and Mick Bunnage

First published 2004 by Boxtree
an imprint of Pan Macmillan Ltd
Pan Macmillan, 20 New Wharf Road, London N1 9RR
Basingstoke and Oxford
Associated companies throughout the world
www.panmacmillan.com

ISBN 978-0-752-22616-3

Text and illustrations copyright © Modern Toss Limited, 2004
PO Box 386, Brighton BN1 3SN, England
www.moderntoss.com
Back cover image: Corbis

9 8 7 6 5 4

A CIP catalogue record for this book is available from the British Library.

Designed and typeset by Modern Toss Limited
Printed and bound in Great Britain by Butler and Tanner

Visit **www.panmacmillan.com** to read more about all our books
and to buy them. You will also find features, author interviews and news
of any author events, and you can sign up for e-newsletters so that you're
always first to hear about our new releases.

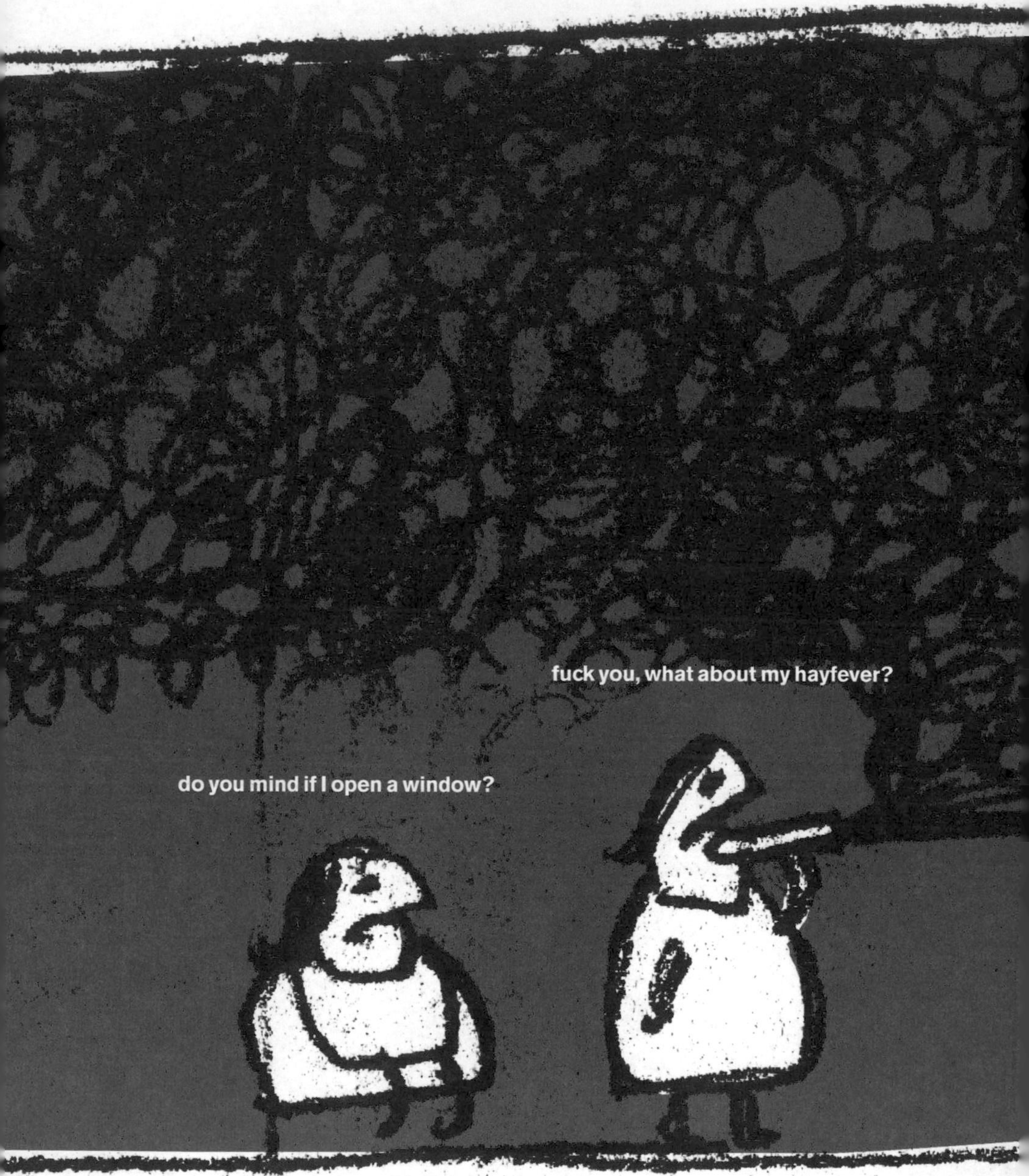
fuck you, what about my hayfever?
do you mind if I open a window?

allergies

work

and what do you think?

are you worried about SARS?

no, I like it I think it's good

999

hello, my dog licked a car battery after I left some meat on top of it...

Mr Tourette

MASTER SIGNWRITER

hello Mr Tourette, can you
paint "Peter's Coffee Shop"
on the side of my van?

mmn, ok

Later...

Oh no, this isn't what I wanted

you're going to have to be a bit more fucking specific

PRINCE EDWARD
~ ROYAL ENTREPRENEUR ~

Mr Tourette

MASTER SIGNWRITER

Later...

i live 'ere

i mashed up some holiday maker good an proper, in fact es's in the boot o me car, i chases im down the field an smacks is ead off wiv me spade he won be makin holidays no more.

I planted is wife in field, she'll be makin no more racket

is car is in me house, i filled it up wiv mud, e won be drivin it up an down no more

i taped is ead on me sky dish... as a warnin

PRINCE EDWARD
~ ROYAL ENTREPRENEUR ~

WESSEX
TURF
SLICES
PISSED
ON BY
ROYAL
HORSES,
PEOPLE
& DOGS

customer services

this book i bought off you, is fucking shit

Dogkiller

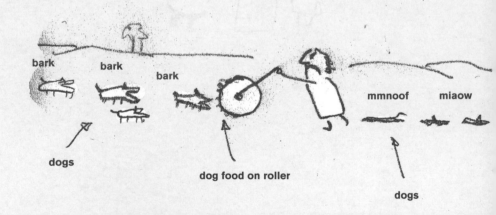

bark   bark   bark   mmnoof   miaow

dogs   dog food on roller   dogs

NATIONAL
PORNOGRAPHIC

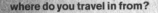

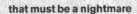

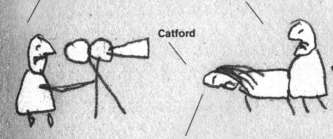

work

i live 'ere

this bloke come to me house for the weekend, said he was a advertising, e offered me 2o fousand for me home, i hit 'is wife wiv a rake, an ven i reversed over em in a tractor an buried em in a lime pit...

CUSTOMER SERVICE

this CD I bought off you, made me kill someone

barbera dickson & slipknot

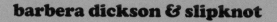

january, february
I don't understand, first
you say you love me

then I fuck your sister, wooaahhh, woooarrrghh

daytrippers

at LINCOLN CATHEDRAL

you did get two kid's tickets didn't you?

No, I smashed up the booth while we were deciding where to go

yeah, if they ask for our tickets, just tell them the truth

yeah, we haven't got any tickets due to vandalism

so what's in Lincoln, have they still got that fucking Cathedral?

yeah, but if we lob a couple of gravestones through the big stained glass window it should come down like a sock

for some reason I always get it mixed up with Coventry

nothing there for us, due to the pioneering work of the Luftwaffe

park

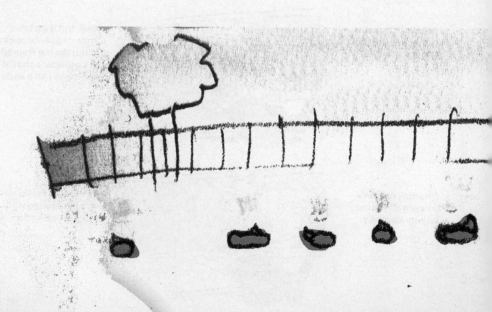

it helps us find our way home

Mr Tourette

MASTER SIGNWRITER

Ahh yes Mr Tourette, I want "Welcome to Merlin's World" with an "e" on the end of world like in the old days

I might try something a bit gothicky, no extra charge

Later...

Piss Wizard

that, is fucking shit

you cunt, this is SO fucking typical

weekend

yeah, having a beer, watching a Hitler documentary

customer
services

this kitchen I bought off you, has given me manic depression

PRINCE EDWARD
~ ROYAL ENTREPRENEUR ~

Gentlemen, welcome to a unique business opportunity

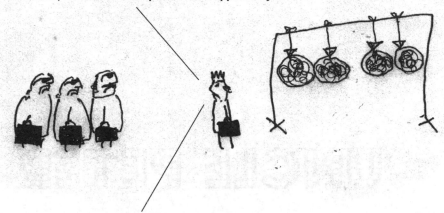

bags of Royal Hair, mainly Princess Margarets

UNCLE PETER

get us an ice cream or we'll eat some dogshit

Mr Tourette

MASTER SIGNWRITER

Oh hello, can you paint "Bob's School of Motoring" on the old car

no sweat

Later...

fucking exactly, you better like it, because I'm not doing it again Grandad

yes... is that what I asked for?

park

that's a long tail

actually it's shit

Mr Tourette

MASTER SIGNWRITER

a poignant moment...

seafoodchain

weekend

so anyway it was quite
incredible, I ring up for a
whore, and who should pick up
the phone at the other end but
Charlotte my wife

that's a fucking coincidence,
exactly the same thing
happend to me and Emma

i
live
'ere

sum bloke cum to
me door selling me
a tea cloff. I say can
I have a look at it,
i tied a knot in it an
whipped his eye out
on ve floor , an trod
on it. then i got a
draw full of cloffs

barber

size

PRINCE EDWARD
~ ROYAL ENTREPRENEUR ~

Prince William's milk teeth, that big one's a tenner

work

I think I'll go home, I'm a bit bored

weekend/Dogkiller

In-season bitch

customer services

this bike I bought off you, ripped my cock off

Indecent Proposal

a hundred pounds to suckle your wife

spider
self-harm
group

I started pulling my legs off when my parents split up

NEXT ISSUE: "A PHONE CALL"

Mr Tourette

MASTER SIGNWRITER

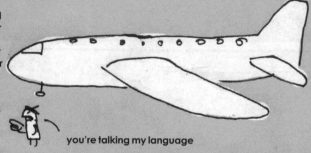

ahh Mr Tourette, we need a brand new livery for our executive city flier jet service, we're looking for a solution that will work for the international market

you're talking my language

Later...

Oh my fucking Christ

SEX TOURISTS

I know what you're thinking, "a bit gloomy"

the archers

I'm not racist, but that refugee camp is going to fuck our chances of best kept village

I caught one of them eating my tree

PRINCE EDWARD
~ ROYAL ENTREPRENEUR ~

you said it would be the Duchess of Kent

pipe down they're just helping him off with his trousers

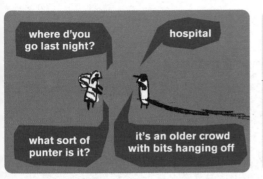

home clubber

charity trees

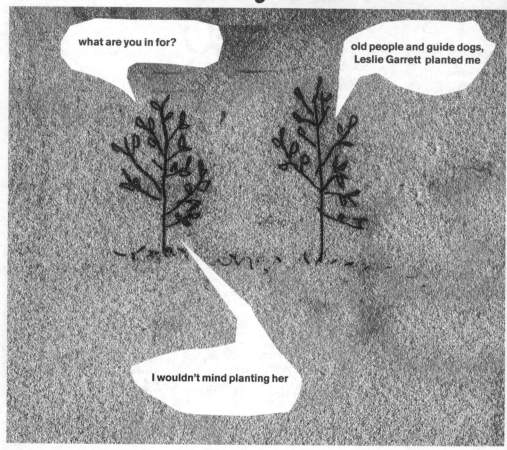

daytrippers

at WINDSOR SAFARI PARK

you're not going to like this, we've only got an hour 'til the coach goes back

I'm not happy about that we'll only be able to do half a job

still, just enough time to snap a pelican and tie it in a reek knot

yeah, I'm going to set fire to some bears

yeah I could smash up the moth cage with an elephant's tusk

I could pump a flamingo up with gas and pierce it with a hammer

In an ideal world I'd like to scoop out a whale with a spade and pump it's jelly into a silverback

yeah well, welcome to the real world, meet back here in 50 minutes

weekend

Let's go to Ikea

fuck Ikea

i live 'ere too

I been up all night burnin' meat, i stripped all ve skin off it to make a boot fer me foot, i used the fat for a blanket, i kept some over to make a hat for my little man, i used a horse leg across ve bottom of me door to keep the ants out, ones at get fru, e waps em wiv a spoon

home clubber

it started off as an old collection of drinks and now it's the UK's premier wasp nightspot

DAVID

GARY

999

I'm arresting you for impersonating a police car

It's a brain tumour you cunt

and what do you think?

are you worried about Genetic Engineering?   yeah, it might extinct me

Mr Tourette

MASTER SIGNWRITER

stick this flag in over there

you fucking do it

SPACE ARGUMENT #1

weekend

That chest of drawers you just delivered is blocking my telly

insect jackass

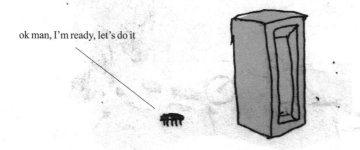

Mr Tourette

MASTER SIGNWRITER

bloody big Air Show on.
Need a banner for the
back of the tiger moth,
can you do it?

yeah I like wars

Later...

HITLER'S COCK

jeeping fuck

yeah it works for me,
I saw one of those crash
into a bus last year

PRINCE EDWARD
~ ROYAL ENTREPRENEUR ~

Queen Mother's last cough, bottled... 50 quid

work

i live 'ere
{election special}

some man cum to me house asking if he can rely on me vote. i say i'll vote for you if you look in me house. e says e's anti europe, he says e can improve the farmin. I stuck a pole fru im, an hanged him from a rafter

Venice Mood

{£845 for 3 days}

Mr Tourette
MASTER SIGNWRITER

Later...

PARK

been Christmas shopping?

no, carrying all their shit around

greeting pipe

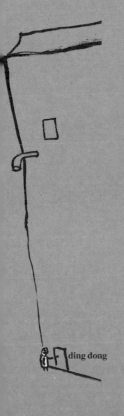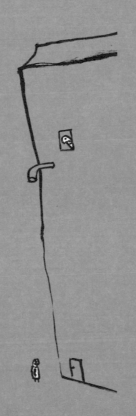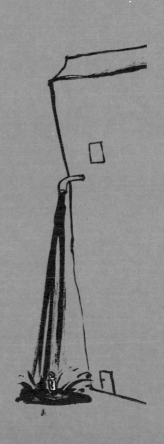

public hanging re-enactment festival

cut her guts out

and at 4.30, we urge you not to miss

the burning of Joan of Arc in the Killing Field next to the car park

PRINCE EDWARD
~ ROYAL ENTREPRENEUR ~

I've had a bloody great idea Edward, really expensive oatmeal biscuits, grown organically in Scotland, and delivered by Royal Stag, I will call them "Monarch's Crust"

yeah whatever, just wank into this old can, I've got a coach load of Japs outside, they've all paid upfront for a royal baby

Mr Tourette

MASTER SIGNWRITER

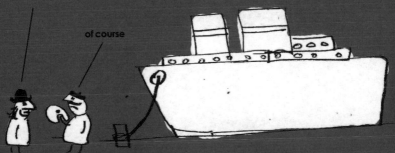

outdoor tv watcher

customer services

this drink I bought off you, made me piss myself

Dogkiller

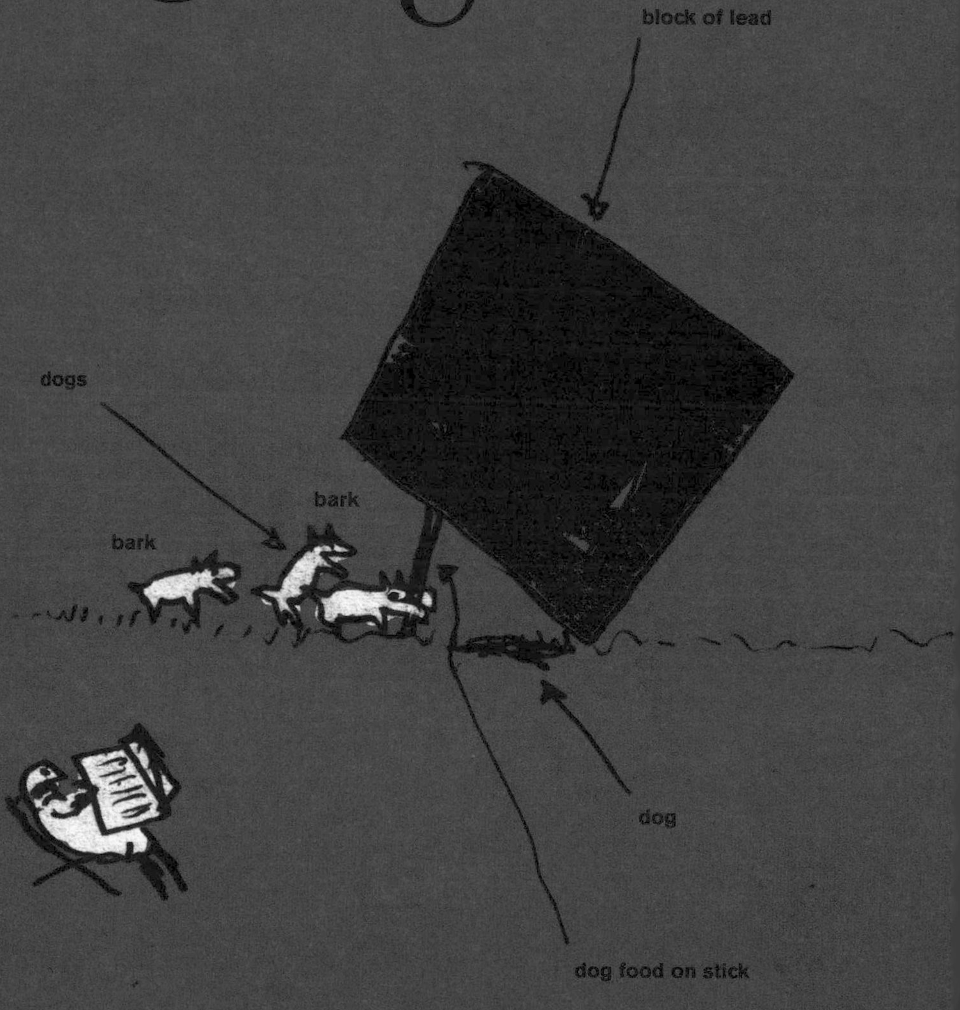

daytrippers

at the Ideal Home Exhibition

are you ready for this Ideal Home Exhibition?

yeah Earls Court innit?

I'm going to let this ground to air FX40 off in soft furnishings

that's going to make a right mess of Gloria Hunniford

might be an improvement, so I see you bought some toxins, what is it? east euro sarin?

yeah picked it up in Calais. Llewellyn Bowen's gonna get a bit of a surprise

that'll blow all his fucking hair out won't it?

Yeah I'm gonna wipe it on him with a shovel. He can't go on telly without a face...

science

pet shop

customer services | 999

I drank all this brown paint thinking it was coffee, now I'm on a life support machine

work

so if i keep not coming in, you're going to start not paying me?

fly
talk

i was in this blokes bedroom he's just gone to sleep, so i thought I'd go over to the window see what it's like outside, next thing i know he's trying to whip my fucking eye out with a vest

I got trapped in Jeremy Iron's house for three weeks, while he fucked off on holiday

HEATWAVE
TOILET

one of your customer's piss
rebounded on my legs

daytrippers

in the Agricultural Show

you all set for this bloody farmer's show then? What's in the bag?

a load of cow food smeared up with tuberculosis

nice, once they've had a dose we can stand them in the organic snacks tent and blow them up

yeah, i'm going to pack a tractor's exhaust with a tube of fox shit and then blast it into a farmers eye

right, I'll coat a steam engine in sugar and plough it into the fertiliser stall, that'll give us a 24 hour burning beacon

good thinking we can work after dark. For the big finish I've given myself mixamatosis,

shame there aren't any rabbits

don't need rabbits, im going to froth up and burn Hugh Fearnley Wittingstall's face off with it.

SPACE ARGUMENT #2

**you sound like a fucking
pig when you eat that**

insect jackass

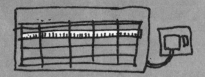

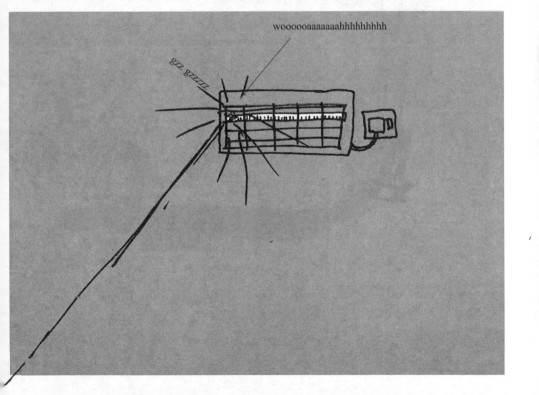

Mr Tourette

MASTER SIGNWRITER

can you paint "HOTDOGS" on my cart, I need something eyecatching there's a lot of competition around

Don't panic, I excel in a competitive business environment

Later...

this better not put people off

what do you mean? they're fucking lapping it up you cunt

fly
talk

I used to fly with this gang yeah.
we used to do the bins round the
back of harrods, one day Nigel
Havers comes out with this fresh
trout, 20,000 of us piled on top of
him, he looked like a big ball of
shit by the time we'd finished

I used to hang around
with Chris Tarrant,
anyway, one day I
managed to worm me
way on to his private jet,
only ended up in fucking
Brazil, can't be bad...

customer services

that expensive food I bought off you has clogged up my drain

daytrippers

at Glastonbury

Are you ready for this shit then?

yeah, I've got a bag full of drugs mostly rat poison

nice this cowboy outfit should make me look like a right cunt

this Police outfit should entitle me to push Peter Gabriel into the piss trench

yeah let's smash the fuck out of a noodle stall

yeah, I'm going to the green field to burst some hippies

I'm going to go backstage and set fire to some drummers

I'm going to find the bloke that runs it and shave his stupid idiot beard off

M'r Tourette,
MASTER SIGNWRITER

these are exciting times at National Delivery Systems, I've got a fleet of vans waiting to be logo'd up with our corporate message

  I am so on your wavelength

Later...

V
A   F
N   U C
SYSTEM
K

I can see where you're going with it, but here's £25 to fuck off

  cheers if you want anything else doing give us a call

Anniversary Meal

I've taken the liberty of ordering something a little bit fucking special

Mr Tourette

MASTER SIGNWRITER

PRINCE EDWARD
~ ROYAL ENTREPRENEUR ~

Listen to this:
"I'm putting together an entertainment benefit
package for orphans, I'm calling it "Electric Blue
Blood - On The Job with the Swedish Royals"
I've sent you a video of the Dutch King to let you
know what I'm after (no animals, it's not selling)
I strongly advise you to fucking do it, or I'll put
your heads on the German one.

cheeky little cunt, is he going to bang it out on the internet?

a poignant moment

solar- powered danger sign

Death Row Chicken

it's finger qwacking good

1. FULL BLOW-OUT
$14.99

12 pieces of Chicken, 4 Regular Fries, 8 spicy Wings, 500ml tub of American Ice Cream, Large tub of BBQ Beans, 1 Bottle of Soft Drink.

2. FAMILY BUCKET
$10.99

8 pieces of Chicken, 4 Regular Fries, 8 spicy wings, 1 Tub of Coleslaw, 1 Tub of Beans, 1 Bottle of Soft Drink.

3. VALUE BOX
$3.99

2 pieces of chicken, 1 Regular Fries, 3 Spicy Wings, 1 Can of Soft Drink.

4. LICK IT UP
$2.99

Chicken Sandwich, 1 Regular Fries, choice of 2 Hot Wings or can of Soft Drink.

5. TWO LOVERS MEAL
$6.99

4 pieces of Chicken and Regular Fries, 4 spicy Wings, BBQ Beans, coleslaw, 2 Cans of Soft Drink.

6. FULL METAL JACKET
$7.99

6 pieces of Chicken, 3 Regular Fries, 1 Tub of Coleslaw, 1 Tub of Beans.

7. NUGGET SURPRISE
$3.49

10 Chicken Nuggets and Dips, 1 Regular Fries, 1 Can of Soft Drink

i'll have the Ho-killer nugget box

do you want a drink with it?

Mr Tourette

could you paint a sign for our exclusive Golf Club set in 200 acres of rolling grassland, we were thinking "The Queens English Country Golfclub"

yeah, I can really get inside the modern business mind

Later...

BUSINESS

PIG

HOLE

should keep the riff raff out

this will put us on the map

you've certainly caught the spirit of the place

you'll probably notice I'm coming at it sideways

daytrippers

at the Albert Hall

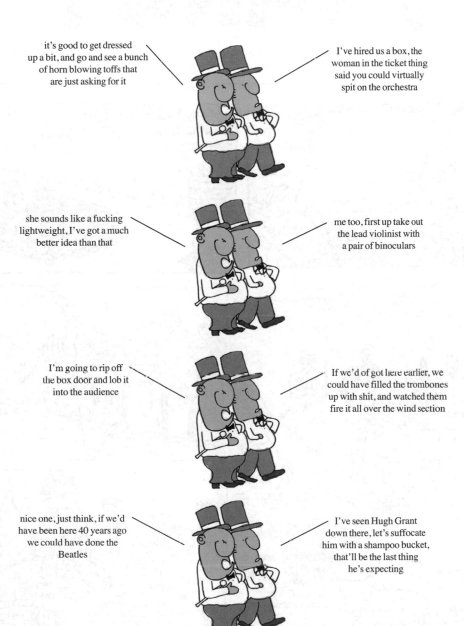

it's good to get dressed up a bit, and go and see a bunch of horn blowing toffs that are just asking for it

I've hired us a box, the woman in the ticket thing said you could virtually spit on the orchestra

she sounds like a fucking lightweight, I've got a much better idea than that

me too, first up take out the lead violinist with a pair of binoculars

I'm going to rip off the box door and lob it into the audience

If we'd of got here earlier, we could have filled the trombones up with shit, and watched them fire it all over the wind section

nice one, just think, if we'd have been here 40 years ago we could have done the Beatles

I've seen Hugh Grant down there, let's suffocate him with a shampoo bucket, that'll be the last thing he's expecting

PEANUT

HAVING DISABLED THEIR MANAGER SPODSIE, DAVID AND PAUL OF MOD SUPERGROUP PEANUT TURN UP AT SINGER GARY'S HOUSE WITH A VIEW TO RESOLVING DIFFICULT BAND ISSUES

DAVID

GARY

PAUL

animal work

hello, yeah I want to invest some of my legmeat in a pension

schlip

SPACE ARGUMENT #3

have you been drinking out of my mug?

MIND YOUR BUSINESS

Dogkiller

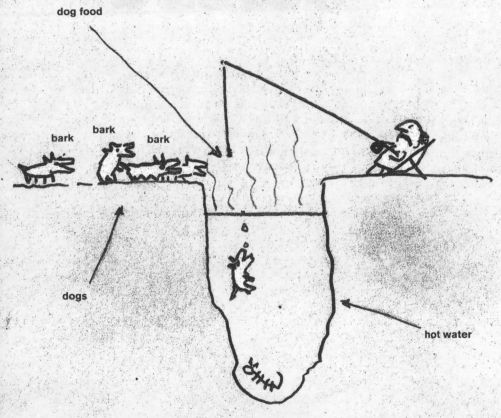

fly
talk

I picked up a virus at Heathrow
airport after licking a piece of ham,
I then got trapped in a cab with
Michael Winner who took me to a
top London restaurant -
I went over to the serving hatch and
honked me guts up on a seabass

yeah I was at this kids party, I'd
just sicked up on a plate of
crisps, then this kid snapped
me leg off and fucked half my
eye out with a cocktail stick

customer services

these pants I bought off you, there's shit in them, but it's not mine, how do I stand legally

Mr Tourette
MASTER SIGNWRITER

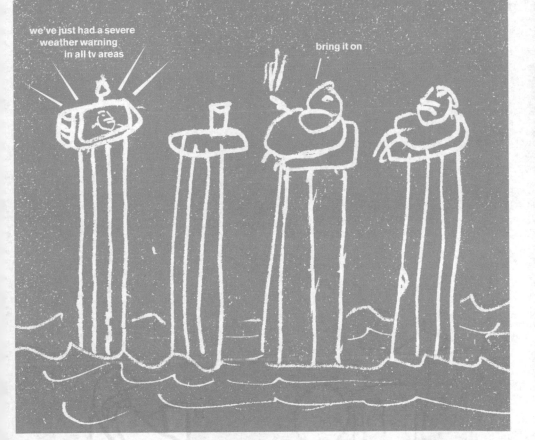

home clubber

I got it off ebay, it used to be Hitler's personal drumkit

work

I've heard the printers broken, so I'm not coming in

SPACE ARGUMENT #4

how the fuck did you manage to tread dog shit on the carpet?

work

right, will anyone who isn't actually a prisoner please go home

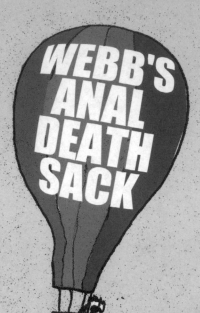